JUNIOR BIOGRAPHY FROM

ANCIENT CIVILIZATIONS

BUDDHA

TAMMY GAGNE

D1606868

Mitchell Lane
PUBLISHERS
2001 SW 31st Avenue
Hallandale, FL 33009
www.mitchelllane.com

JUNIOR BIOGRAPHY FROM ANCIENT CIVILIZATIONS

**Alexander the Great • Archimedes • Augustus Caesar
Buddha • Charlemagne • Cleopatra • Confucius
Genghis Khan • Hammurabi • Hippocrates • Homer
Julius Caesar • King Arthur • Leif Erikson • Marco Polo
Moses • Nero • Plato • Pythagoras • Socrates**

Copyright © 2018 by Mitchell Lane Publishers

Printing 1 2 3 4 5 6 7 8 9

ABOUT THE AUTHOR: Tammy Gagne is the author of numerous books for adults and children, including *Cleopatra* and *Charlemagne* for Mitchell Lane Publishers. She resides in northern New England with her husband and son. One of her favorite pastimes is visiting schools to speak to kids about the writing process.

PUBLISHER'S NOTE: The facts on which the story in this book is based have been thoroughly researched. Documentation of such research can be found on pages 44–45. While every possible effort has been made to ensure accuracy, the publisher will not assume liability for damages caused by inaccuracies in the data, and makes no warranty on the accuracy of the information contained herein.

To reflect current usage, we have chosen to use the secular era designations BCE ("before the common era") and CE ("of the common era") instead of the traditional designations BC ("before Christ") and AD (*anno Domini,* "in the year of the Lord").

Library of Congress Cataloging-in-Publication Data

Names: Gagne, Tammy, author.
Title: Buddha / by Tammy Gagne.
Description: Hallandale, FL : Mitchell Lane Publishers, 2018. | Series: Junior biography from ancient civilizations | Includes bibliographical references and index.
Identifiers: LCCN 2017009112 | ISBN 9781680200140 (library bound)
Subjects: LCSH: Gautama Buddha—Juvenile literature.
Classification: LCC BQ892 .G34 2017 | DDC 294.3/63 [B] —dc23
LC record available at https://lccn.loc.gov/2017009112

eBook ISBN: 978-1-618020-015-7

CONTENTS

Phonetic pronunciations of words in **bold**
can be found on page 46.

King Sudhodana wanted his son Siddhartha to take over his throne one day. The prince would end up taking a very different path, however. Instead of ruling the kingdom of Kapilavastu, Siddhartha would become the founder of an entire religion.

The Awakening

He was born as the prince of a small kingdom in India. As he grew up, he had everything most young men desired: enormous wealth, a beautiful wife, and a newborn son to carry on his royal legacy. In addition, his father King **Sudhodana*** had been preparing him to become the next king. The king even built three palaces for him: one for cold weather, one for hot weather, and a third for use during the rainy season. Still, **Siddhartha Gautama** felt something vital was missing in his life. He tried his hardest to meet his family's expectations. But he knew he had a different calling.

He was already a grown man when he ventured outside his palace walls for the first time. When he did, he "witnessed people suffering from sickness, weakened by old age, and being dumped in charnel grounds after death. It became clear to him that he could not reconcile his life inside the palace and the suffering outside its walls,"[1] states journalist Thomas Graves.

One night as his wife and infant son slept, Siddhartha took one last look at them before

*For pronunciations of words in **bold**, see page 46.

leaving the palace for good. It is said that he didn't wake them for fear that he might change his mind. But in his heart, Siddhartha knew that remaining a husband, a father, and a prince would keep him from fulfilling his true purpose.

In an effort to fulfill this purpose, he spent several years wandering throughout a vast area of northern India. What did he do during this time? And did he find the path that he was seeking?

As journalist Carol Brozozowski explains, "He started out with traditional Hindu [the dominant religion in India] practices, which he found empty."[2] He then tried more severe acts, fasting until his hair fell out. He soon realized such behaviors were pointless. So he began to focus on meditating—a deep process that some call the quieting of the mind. He hoped it would bring him closer to the answers he was seeking.

Through meditation Siddhartha eventually reached the stage of enlightenment. This highest state of being—of awakening to the truth—was what he had been seeking all along. Legend states that this wondrous event took place as he meditated under the Bodhi tree in Bodh Gaya, a small town in India. At this point Siddhartha became known as Buddha, which means "the enlightened one."

Buddha at Bodh Gaya

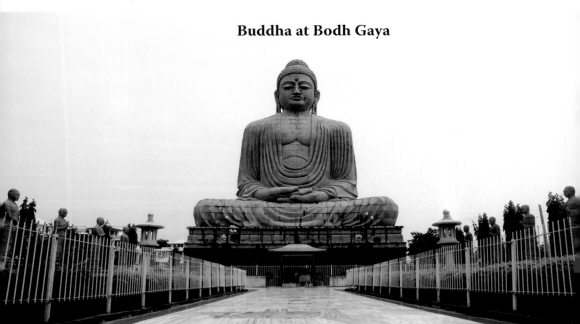

Today a monument called the Mahabodhi Temple stands in Bodh Gaya. It marks the spot where Buddha is said to have achieved enlightenment.

A Buddhist monk named Ananda planted the Anandabodhi tree at the Jetavana Monastery. It began as a sapling of the Mahabodi tree Buddha sat under in Bodh Gaya. Today it is considered one of the holiest trees in Buddhism.

Buddha claimed that human suffering was linked to the cycle of rebirth. Both Hindus and Buddhists believe that all human beings live over and over again through a process called reincarnation. A person's next life is said to be determined by karma—the quality of his or her thoughts and actions in this life. If people are kind and generous, they will be rewarded with a better life the next time around. But if they are cruel and greedy, they will suffer more in their next life.

After reaching enlightenment, Buddha's work was just beginning. He wanted to share his knowledge with others. He "gathered disciples to his life of homelessness and missionary service," says Brozozowski. "His teachings were aimed at ordinary people."[3] He saw human beings—of both high birth and low birth, rich and poor, young and old—as the key to changing the world.

Today Buddhism has about three hundred million followers. While they greatly admire the former prince who devoted his life to ending human suffering, they do not worship him. Instead, they follow the path that he forged. "Buddha himself is considered a human above other humans, but not a god,"[4] Brozozowski concludes.

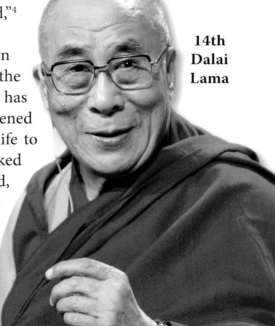

14th Dalai Lama

One of the best known Buddhists is the Dalai Lama, the Tibetan spiritual leader. He has never even claimed to be enlightened himself. He simply devotes his life to compassion for others. When asked about Buddhism, he has answered, "My religion is kindness." He has also pointed out that following his religion is simple. "No need for temples," he says. "Your own mind, your own heart is the temple."[5]

What Did Buddha Look Like?

According to journalist Sara Wise, "We, the unenlightened, tend to think of Buddha as a chubby little man sitting cross-legged, a wide grin above a pot belly"[6] This image is largely due to the countless number of sculptures of the spiritual leader found throughout the world today. But other descriptions of him differ greatly from this popular image.

For example, author Jack Kerouac wrote, "People didn't know that the actual Buddha was a handsome young prince who cut off his long golden hair with his sword."[7]

Buddha was said to reject idols made in his image. "The Buddha had, after all, told his followers not to worship him in image, that adoration was not the route to enlightenment,"[8] adds Wise. Perhaps this is why more than 400 Buddha statues were buried under the site of a Buddhist temple near Beijing, China. The figures, which were discovered in 1996, had been placed in a large pit between 1100 and 1150. And they were already more than five hundred years old at that time.

No matter why the sculptures were hidden, however, they offered a different view of the Buddhist master. "These Buddhas," notes Wise, "are petite and slender, with gently curving . . . torsos, rosebud mouths and long, fine noses."[9]

Art depicting Buddha and his family can be found around the world today. This statue of Queen Mayadevi, Buddha's mother, is on display at the Guimet Museum in Paris. It was created in Nepal during the 19th century.

CHAPTER 2
A Master is Born

Though historians have been studying Buddha for centuries, no one knows exactly when he was born. The best clues about his life have been found in the ancient texts written about him. From these early writings, historians guess that Buddha lived about 2,500 years ago. He was most likely born around 563 BCE in the foothills of the Himalayan Mountains in either modern-day India or Nepal.

In the documentary *The Life of Buddha*, an Indian storyteller shares the tale of Buddha's birth. "Ten months before the birth of her child, Queen **Mayadevi** had a strange dream. A white elephant with six tusks, its head painted red, entered into her body," he says. "And it stayed there like a precious stone. King Sudhodana called the astrologers. They said that the dream told of the birth of an extraordinarily great master."[1]

As the prince's birth neared, the queen prepared to travel to Nepal because of a long-standing tradition that a woman should give birth to her first child in her parents' home. Mayadevi was on her way there when she came upon a village called Lumbini. It was late summer, and the mother-to-be was hot and tired. When she saw a huge tree with beautiful leaves, she decided it was the perfect spot to stop and rest for a while. The queen also noticed a nearby pond where she could bathe. While she was in the water, her labor pains began. According to the story, the young prince was soon born in that very village.

Following the child's birth, the queen returned to the king and their kingdom in the city of **Kapilavastu**. This was the capital city of the Sakya people. The couple named their new son Siddhartha, which means "the one who brings all good."[2] The entire kingdom joined them in celebrating the baby's birth. People came from all over to welcome the prince.

Today Lumbini is known as Buddha's birthplace. People from both near and far come to see the pond in which Queen Mayadevi bathed before giving birth to her prince.

Before he became known as Buddha, Prince Siddhartha Gautama walked away from his life of riches and power. At the age of 29, he left his father's royal palace in the middle of the night through this gate.

"One of these visitors was the holy sage, Asita," writes author Gabriel Arquilevich. "Asita told the parents that the prince would be either a great king or a great saint. Then something strange happened. When Asita's eyes met the infant's, the sage began to weep. This worried the king and queen, but Asita explained that these were bittersweet tears he shed for himself, for he saw that this indeed was a special child, one who could lead others to peace."[3]

Asita added that the boy would one day have to make a choice. If he remained in the palace, he could grow up to become a great king. But if he chose a religious path, he could free the world from suffering.

Sadly, the queen would not live to witness her son's future—not even his childhood. Just seven days after Siddhartha's arrival, his mother lay dying. Wanting her son to have a caregiver who loved him, the queen asked her sister, **Pajapati Gotami**, to take over her role as his mother. Following Mayadevi's death, King Sudhodana fulfilled her dying wish by marrying her sister. Siddhartha's aunt was now also his stepmother.

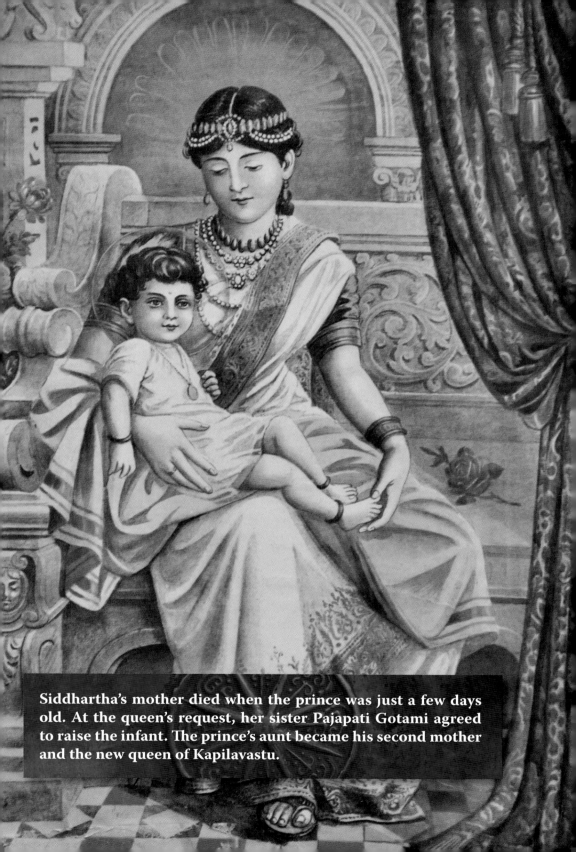

Siddhartha's mother died when the prince was just a few days old. At the queen's request, her sister Pajapati Gotami agreed to raise the infant. The prince's aunt became his second mother and the new queen of Kapilavastu.

Despite the loss of his wife, the king was still mindful of Asita's prediction. Arquievich continues, "Sudhodana wanted to be certain that his son became a great emperor, not a saint. Therefore, he set out to give Siddhartha all he could desire."[4]

The king ordered the construction of a high wall around the palace. When it was finished, he demanded that the builders make it even taller. The wall's door alone was so big and heavy that it needed 16 people to open it. But would this fortification and all the riches be enough to keep the prince within the kingdom?

According to the legends about him, Siddhartha's actions showed him to be remarkable from the beginning of his life. People say that he took his first steps—seven of them—when he was just a newborn. Wherever he placed his tiny feet, lotus flowers appeared. It is said that they grew out of nowhere to protect the baby's delicate feet from the ground.

One sunny July day, Siddhartha's family was working in the fields. Taking the young prince with them, they set him under a nearby tree. Late in the day as they walked home, they realized they had left the little boy behind.

The boy Siddhartha rising up from a lotus

As they ran back to fetch him, his worried family members noticed something odd. As happened every day, the setting sun had caused all the shadows to shift from their original positions—all but one, that is. Siddhartha was still sitting in the same spot of shade that had shielded him many hours earlier. It was as if the sun itself was protecting him. The prince seemed completely unaware that he had been forgotten. He was as unaware of the passing of time as he was of his family's return. When they reached him, Siddhartha was kneeling, meditating for the first time.

Marking the Spot

A major discovery relating to Buddha's birth came in 1996. A group of archaeologists found an unusual stone in Lumbini, Nepal. They believed it marked the spot of Siddhartha's birth. The stone sat on top of a platform with seven layers of brick beneath it. Over the next six months, scientists studied the bricks, proving they dated to the era of Emperor **Ashoka**. He ruled over much of the Indian subcontinent in ancient times and came to Lumbini in 249 BCE. Known for converting from Hinduism to Buddhism, Ashoka is credited with introducing the religion to the nations of eastern Asia.

Following the discovery, the *St. Petersburg Times* explained, "Buddhist literature says Ashoka placed a stone on top of bricks at the birthplace and also built a nearby pillar that still stands."[5] An inscription on the pillar claims the spot as the birthplace of Buddha.

Birthplace of Buddha

For centuries people had debated whether Buddha had been born in Nepal or in India. Some historians regard this find as clear evidence that Nepal was indeed his rightful birthplace. Nepal's prime minister declared, "It is a matter of pride for all of us that the sacred birthplace of Lord Buddha has been discovered."[6]

Most sculptures of Buddha show him as an adult. This one from an Asian garden, however, depicts him as a young child.

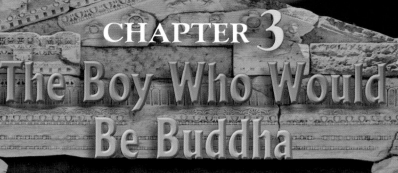

CHAPTER 3
The Boy Who Would Be Buddha

Even as a young boy, Siddhartha was wise and compassionate. His father wanted him to have the best possible education. It is said that Siddhartha learned to read and write after only a few lessons. Some legends claim that he even spoke several languages before ever going to school.

India was home to many different religions during Siddhartha's early years. His family followed the Vedas, the teachings of the Hindu faith. The young prince would join this religion as well. As *The Life of Buddha* explains, "When he turned six, he was subjected to a traditional ritual. They adorned him with beautiful clothes and ornaments and took him to the temple to worship. His stepmother, Queen Gotami, said, 'Now we should formally initiate him into our family tradition. He must go through the childbirth ritual. We should take him to our family deity— stick to our family tradition.'"[1]

The prince's family had no idea what awaited them at the temple. It is said that when they entered with Siddhartha, all the statues of the

A bronze statue of
Buddha and a swan

Devadutta did not like his cousin Siddhartha's ways. The above image shows an elephant that Devadutta drugged and released, hoping it would harm his young cousin. Instead, Siddhartha was able to win over the intoxicated beast with kindness.

gods stood up out of respect for the holy child. Each one proceeded to bow down in front of him.

It would have been easy for Siddhartha to feel vain or entitled. The many benefits that his father's position and wealth provided him would have spoiled most children. But Siddhartha remained overwhelmingly peaceful and kind. He lived in a palace filled with marble statues and monuments. But he didn't care about owning expensive objects. And he wasn't fond of fighting, as his cousin **Devadutta** was.

Devadutta enjoyed practicing to become a warrior. He didn't understand why his cousin did not share in his enthusiasm. He saw Siddhartha as being disrespectful of their family's way.

One morning, Devadutta used his bow to shoot a swan out of the sky. With the arrow stuck in its wing, the bird plummeted into a palace garden where Siddhartha was playing. According to the *New Indian Express*, "Without hesitation Siddhartha pulled out the arrow. 'There, it's removed now,' he whispered softly to the bird, stroking its head. 'Let's see how we mend you.' Gathering some herbs from the garden he made a paste and applied it to the bleeding wound. Then tearing off a piece of his upper garment, he wrapped the swan gently with it."[2]

When Devadutta came to fetch his kill, he saw that Siddhartha was nursing it back to health. The young archer was furious. He demanded that Siddhartha hand over the bird, reminding him that the law of the land stated that the hunter owned any animal he had killed. Siddhartha refused.

Devadutta could hardly believe that his gentle cousin wasn't backing down. He was clearly more stubborn than Devadutta realized. The two boys took their dispute to the king's court.

At first it seemed that Kapilavastu's law was on Devadutta's side. But when Siddhartha pointed out that the swan was not dead, the ministers agreed that he, not Devadutta, should keep the bird. The young prince only kept the swan long enough for its wound to heal.

"After a few weeks Siddhartha brought the swan, now fully recovered, into the garden," continues the *New Indian Express*. "Holding it gently in his hands, he opened his palms. 'Go, my friend! It's time for you to join your companions!' The swan flapped its wings and soared up. Suddenly from nowhere, appeared two more swans. They had come to lead him home."[3]

Did That Really Happen?

Many people regard the stories of Siddhartha's early years as mere legends—myths made up to show Buddha's enormous compassion. In the book *Buddha: A Very Short Introduction*, author Michael Carrithers writes, "Later traditions [exaggerated] a great deal of the Buddha's early life, but of this we can rely on little."[4] The stories created clear pictures of the boy, and later the man. "But since such images were not made until centuries after his death they cannot be portraits,"[5] Carrithers adds. He isn't saying that the stories are untrue. But he does stress that no one can prove they actually happened.

Many devoted Buddhists insist that the legends about Buddha's life describe events that actually took place. The fact that the stories were not recorded in writing for hundreds of years does not lessen their belief in them. These followers point out that the stories were passed down from one generation to the next over the centuries. They also see that believing them is an act of their faith.

Not all Buddhists feel they must take all the stories about Buddha literally, though. These followers believe deeply in Buddhism. But they accept the stories about Buddha as instruments for explaining the Buddhist faith.

Young Buddhist monks praying in front of the Buddha image in Wat Suan Dok temple in Chiang Mai, Thailand

When it came time for Prince Siddhartha to choose a wife, he had many choices. The young prince took his time making this important decision. He would only marry a woman who proved to be of the highest character.

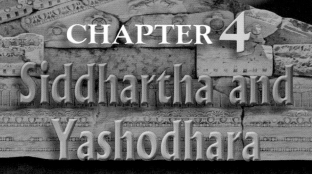

CHAPTER 4
Siddhartha and Yashodhara

When Siddhartha turned sixteen, his father expected him to choose a wife. This was the traditional age for a young man of this era to marry. But for the son of a king, the selection process was quite different from the way common men selected their brides.

It was said that the king invited more than 4,000 unmarried girls to meet Siddhartha. He believed that his son could certainly find one young woman he liked from among this great number. Many young men would have been delighted to have such a selection of possible brides. But Siddhartha told his father that he would only marry a girl who possessed the qualities most important to him.

The young prince had high standards for the woman he would choose. In addition to possessing a high moral character, he also wanted her to be young and pretty. But Siddhartha insisted, "Her youth will not make her vain, nor will her beauty make her proud. She whom I shall marry will have a sister's affection, a mother's tenderness, for all living creatures. She will be sweet and truthful, and she will not know envy. Never, not even in her dreams, will she think of any other man but her husband."[1] He also did not want someone who was easily influenced by music or drama. And she wouldn't drink wine or eat sweets. He wanted someone who was kind to both him and others—even those who served her.

Finding a young woman who fulfilled his long list of expectations would not be easy. Throughout the ceremony, Siddhartha met girl after girl. He treated each one with great courtesy and respect. But none of them stood out as the one he wanted to become his wife.

Near the end of the ceremony, though, he noticed an especially beautiful young woman. The daughter of a nearby king, she was named **Yashodhara**. Because the young women had come to meet him, the prince had the responsibility of giving them each a gift. When he began handing them out, Yashodhara was the only one who did not step forward. He asked her why she didn't want her gift. She explained that she already had everything she needed.

Siddhartha was so impressed by Yashodhara's unselfishness that he offered her his own diamond necklace. The people took this grand gesture as a sign of his affection for the girl. It seemed the prince had finally chosen his wife.

The girl's father, King **Dandapani**, was not so quick to accept the match, however. He saw Siddhartha as being unworthy of his daughter. After all,

Prince Siddhartha's marriage to Princess Yashodhara took place at King Sudhodana's Golden Palace. People celebrated the event with the royal family for many days.

the prince did not follow in the footsteps of the warrior princes and kings who preceded him. Dandapani thought Siddhartha knew nothing.

To convince Dandapani to give his blessing for the marriage, Sudhodana organized a great tournament. The contest would offer Siddhartha the chance to show off his intelligence and skills in such activities as archery and riding horses.

The contests began with mathematics. Even when given the most difficult problems, "never once was Siddhartha at a loss for the correct solution," according to biographer Andre Ferdinand Herold. "They all marveled at his knowledge of mathematics and were convinced that his intelligence had probed to the bottom of all the sciences. They then decided to challenge his athletic skill, but at jumping and at running he won with little effort, and at wrestling he had only to lay a finger upon his adversary, and he would fall to the ground."[2]

In another event, Siddhartha was pitted against Dandapani's most talented archers. "They placed their arrows in targets that were barely visible," continues Herold. "But when it came the prince's turn to shoot, so great was his natural strength that he broke each bow as he drew it. Finally, the king sent guards to fetch a very ancient, very precious bow that was kept in the temple. No one within the memory of man had ever been able to draw or lift it. Siddhartha took the bow in his left hand, and with one finger of his right hand he drew it to him. Then he took as target a tree so distant that he alone could see it. The arrow pierced the tree, and, burying itself in the ground, disappeared."[3]

When the tournament ended, King Dandapani admitted that he had been wrong about Siddhartha. He apologized to the prince. And he finally gave him his blessing to marry Yashodhara.

A Love of Many Lifetimes

Today many people debate whether Buddha married for love. Some argue that he married only because his father insisted on it. But others view Siddhartha's connection to Yashodhara as so strong that it spanned several lifetimes. One of the major elements of Buddhism is the belief in reincarnation. This idea that people and animals all live many lifetimes is found in legends about Buddha himself.

In a book that some scholars have called the closest text to Buddha's own words, spiritual teacher and translator Eknath Easwaran writes, "Passionately in love with each other, the chronicles say, Prince Siddhartha and Princess Yashodhara had been together for many lives. Their devotion to one another is the supreme example not of selfish attachment but of selfless love. The Jakata stories [part of the ancient Buddhist texts] tell how in former lives, when the Buddha was a tiger, Yashodhara was a tigress; when he was king of the deer, she was the queen. In life after life they came together, and so it was not chance that when the Buddha-to-be was born as a prince in the kingdom of the Shakyas, Yashodhara was born a princess in a kingdom nearby."[4]

Princess Yashodhara places garlands around Siddhartha's neck.

When Siddhartha left his kingdom in the middle of the night, he rode away on his horse, Kanthak. This image shows the young prince and his horse on that fateful night.

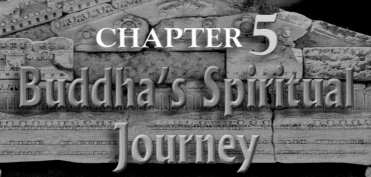

CHAPTER 5
Buddha's Spiritual Journey

For thirteen years after his marriage, Siddhartha continued to live in Kapilavastu as a prince and a husband. During an eclipse, he became a father. When Yashodhara gave birth to a baby boy, the couple named their son **Rahula**. Meaning both "eclipse" and "obstacle," the name strikes some people as a sign of Siddhartha's impending departure.

Over the years he had grown more and more frustrated with his life in the kingdom. He especially disapproved of the caste system that ruled society. This hierarchy stated that a person's position in life was determined by the family into which he or she was born. The higher the level of a family, the higher its caste. Siddhartha thought the system was unfair—that all people should be treated as equals.

Siddhartha struggled with what he should do about his frustrating life. But ultimately, he decided that the only way he would achieve enlightenment was to leave his kingdom and his family. As he moved from one region to the next following his departure, he learned about the

As Rahula grew older, his mother encouraged him to ask for his rightful inheritance. She saw the riches Siddharta had left behind as belonging to their son. Buddha, on the other hand, wanted to bestow a spiritual inheritance to Rahula. He asked his followers to ordain the boy.

various religions of the area. It is said that he studied with six different masters on his journey. But none of these faiths satisfied him.

He realized the only way he would find the answers he sought was to abandon all existing religions. He decided to meditate until he reached enlightenment, also known as nirvana. Six years after he had left Kapilavastu, he finally reached this extraordinary goal.

Buddha, as he was now known, was said to have supreme knowledge. And he wanted to share all he had learned with others. He began by giving a sermon on the Four Noble Truths. The PBS video series *The Living Edens* explains, "The Four Noble Truths comprise the essence of Buddha's teachings, though they leave much to be explained. They are the truth of suffering, the truth of the cause

This painting shows four messengers Siddhartha encountered during his search for enlightenment. An old man, a sick man, a corpse, and a wandering monk were all part of Buddha's spiritual journey.

of suffering, the truth of the end of suffering, and the truth of the path that leads to the end of suffering. More simply put, suffering exists: it has a cause, it has an end, and it has a cause to bring about its end."[1]

These Buddhist truths became known as the Dharma. Buddha traveled far, sharing the Dharma with everyone willing to listen to his teachings. It didn't matter to him if a person was male or female,

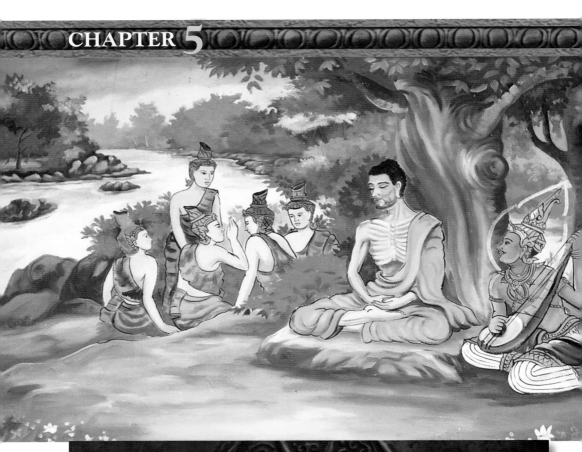

Siddhartha spent a great deal of time meditating while striving to attain his enlightenment. Five monks accompanied him on parts of this journey. They would later become his first students. This painting depicts the Buddha-to-be with those monks and a god who helped him along the way.

young or old, rich or poor. He wanted everyone to know that all people were born as equals—there was no predetermined hierarchy. And he practiced what he preached by treating each person he encountered the same way he treated everyone else.

Buddha insisted that the only way one person could be viewed as better than another was by judging that person's actions. A good person was someone who treated others with kindness and compassion. The only low people were those who treated others badly.

For more than forty years, the Buddha spread his teachings throughout the land. When he reached the age of eighty, he knew his life was coming to an end. On his deathbed, he delivered his last sermon. Called the Nirvana Sutra, it explained that death was not real.

He compared death to a cloud. "When you look at a cloud, you think of the cloud as being," he said. "And later on when the cloud becomes the rain, you don't see the cloud anymore and you say the cloud is not there. And you describe the cloud as non-being. But if you look deeply, you can see the cloud in the rain. And that is why it is impossible for a cloud to die. A cloud can become rain or snow or ice. But a cloud cannot become nothing. And that is why the notion of death cannot be applied to reality . . . whether to a cloud or a human being."[2]

Even the Buddha's last words inspired others to seek enlightenment. "Every man is his own prison," he said before taking his last breath. "But every man can obtain the right to escape. Never stop struggling,"[3] he urged his followers.

Buddha lived a long life on earth. His teachings would endure down to the present day as the foundation of the religion of Buddhism.

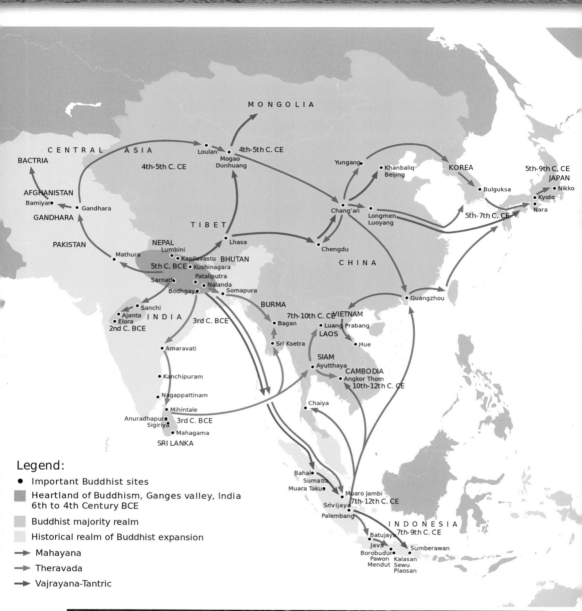

Legend:

- **Important Buddhist sites**
- ■ Heartland of Buddhism, Ganges valley, India 6th to 4th Century BCE
- ■ Buddhist majority realm
- ■ Historical realm of Buddhist expansion
- → Mahayana
- → Theravada
- → Vajrayana-Tantric

Buddhism began in the heartland of northern India during the sixth century BCE. It expanded throughout the Asian continent and eventually reached every corner of the world.

The Caste System Today

Some people are surprised to learn that the caste system still exists in India to this day. "There are four 'main' castes," writes author Walter Henry Nelson, "perhaps as many as two thousand may be said to exist! Within each one of the main four castes, there are members who will look up to others within their caste, and look down upon still others."[4]

Nelson points out that many people use the concept of reincarnation to explain the caste system's survival. They see everyone's position as a matter of cause and effect. "Indians justify the caste system partly on the basis of their belief in rebirth," he states. "What misfortune befalls [a person] in this life he regards as a clear effect of neglected duties in a previous incarnation."[5]

The lowest members of today's caste system are the Dalits, who often perform menial jobs that no one else wants. Over the last 50 years, the Indian government has worked to improve opportunities for this group, which makes up about 20 percent of the country's population. "But in many rural areas," notes journalist Siddhartha Kumar, "Dalits still face discrimination. They are not allowed to enter places of worship and have separate wells for drawing water."[6]

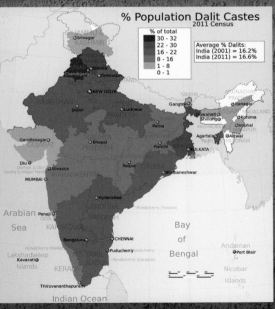

% Population Dalit Castes
2011 Census

% of total
30 - 32
22 - 30
16 - 22
8 - 16
1 - 8
0 - 1

Average % Dalits:
India (2001) = 16.2%
India (2011) = 16.6%

The above map shows how many members of the Dalit caste exist in India today. The largest number are found in the state of Punjab. India's island territories, on the other hand, have no Dalits.

CHRONOLOGY

All dates **BCE** and are estimates based on best available evidence

564	Mayadevi has an odd and wondrous dream.
563	Prince Siddhartha Gautama is born.
557	Siddhartha is introduced to the Hindu faith.
547	The prince marries Yashodhara.
534	Yashodhara gives birth to a son, Rahula.
533	Siddhartha leaves his kingdom in search of enlightenment and wanders for five years.
528	Siddhartha reaches enlightenment and becomes a Buddha.
528-483	Buddha shares his knowledge with others throughout India.
483	Buddha dies at the age of 80.

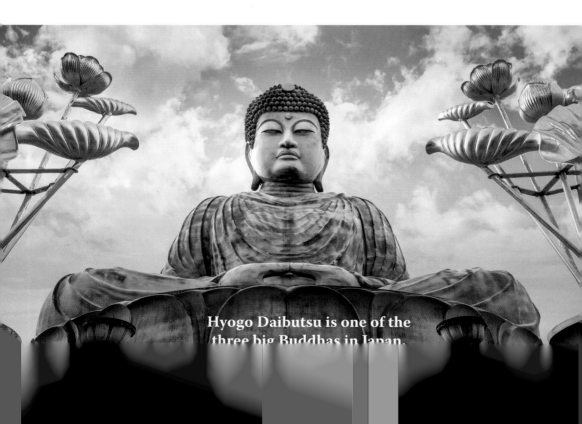

Hyogo Daibutsu is one of the three big Buddhas in Japan.

DATES BCE

ca. 1500	Hinduism begins.
ca. 1300	Judaism is founded.
551	Chinese philosopher Confucius is born.
550	Cyrus the Great founds the Persian Empire.
469	Greek philosopher Socrates is born.
427	Greek philosopher Plato is born.
327	Alexander the Great invades India.
ca. 260	Emperor Ashoka converts to Buddhism.
ca. 220	Construction begins on the Great Wall of China.
100	Roman leader Julius Caesar is born.

DATES CE

ca. 4	Jesus of Nazareth is born.
ca. 30	Christianity begins.
312	Roman Emperor Constantine converts to Christianity.
476	The Western Roman Empire falls.
570	The Prophet Muhammad is born.
ca. 610	Muhammad founds the religion of Islam.
742	The future Holy Roman Emperor Charlemagne is born.
749	The first Buddhist monastery is built in Tibet.
868	The first printed book in world history is created in China.
1054	The Roman Catholic Church and Eastern Orthodox Church formally separate.
1517	Martin Luther's 95 Theses attack contemporary church practices and lead to the establishment of Protestantism.

Chapter 1: The Awakening
1. Thomas Graves, "Buddha's day, 25 centuries later." *The Sun* (Baltimore), May 2, 1988.
2. Carol Brozozowski, "Beginnings of Buddhism." *Sun Sentinel*, August 19, 1988.
3. Ibid.
4. Ibid.
5. T.K. Barger, "You can go far in this world on kindness." *The Blade*, March 8, 2014.
6. Sarah Wise, "Saturday review: Arts—Secrets of the Buddha." *The Guardian*, April 27, 2002.
7. Jack Kerouac, *Wake Up* (New York: Viking, 2008 [reprint]), p. 9.
8. Wise, "Saturday review."
9. Ibid.

Chapter 2: A Master Is Born
1. Martin Meissonnier (director), *The Life of Buddha*. Arte, 2004.
2. Gabriel Arquilevich, *World Religions* (Westminster, CA: Teacher Created Resources, 2004), p. 170.
3. Ibid.
4. Ibid.
5. ———. "Birthplace of Buddha is found in Nepal, archaeologists say." *St. Petersburg Times*, February 6, 1996.
6. Ibid.

Chapter 3: The Boy Who Would Be Buddha

1. Martin Meissonnier (director), *The Life of Buddha*. Arte, 2004.
2. ———. "Siddhartha and the Wounded Swan." *The New Indian Express*, June 13, 2014.
3. Ibid.
4. Michael Carrithers, *Buddha: A Very Short Introduction* (Oxford, England: Oxford University Press, 2001), p. 12.
5. Ibid.

Chapter 4: Siddhartha and Yashodhara

1. Andre Ferdinand Herold, *The Life of Buddha*. Amazon Digital Services, 2010, pp. 29-30.
2. Ibid., p. 36.
3. Ibid.
4. Eknath Easwaran, *Essence of the Dhammapada: The Buddha's Call to Nirvana* (Tomales, CA: Nilgiri Press, 2013), p. 141.

Chapter 5: Buddha's Spiritual Journey

1. PBS, *The Living Edens*. http://www.pbs.org/edens/thailand/buddhism.htm
2. Martin Meissonnier (director), *The Life of Buddha*. Arte, 2004.
3. Ibid.
4. Walter Henry Nelson, *Buddha: His Life and His Teaching* (New York: Penguin, 1996), p. 21.
5. Ibid.
6. Siddhartha Kumar, "India to hold caste-based census next year." *McClatchy-Tribune Business News*, September 9, 2010.

Books

Cowhey, Mary. *Black Ants and Buddhists*. Portland, ME: Stenhouse Press, 2006.

Gedney, Mona K. *The Life & Times of Buddha*. Hockessin, DE: Mitchell Lane Publishers, 2005.

Landaw, Jonathan. *Prince Siddhartha: The Story of Buddha*. Somerville, MA: Wisdom Publications, 2011.

Johnson-Weider, Michelle L. *In the Garden of Our Minds and Other Buddhist Stories*. Silver Spring, MD: Blue Moon Aurora, 2013.

Nanji, Shenaaz. *Indian Tales*. Cambridge, MA: Barefoot Books, 2013.

Works Consulted

———. "Birthplace of Buddha is found in Nepal, archaeologists say." *St. Petersburg Times*, February 6, 1996.

———. "Siddhartha and the Wounded Swan." *The New Indian Express*, June 13, 2014.

Armstrong, Karen. *Buddha*. New York: Penguin, 2001.

Arquilevich, Gabriel. *World Religions*. Westminster, CA: Teacher Created Resources, 2004.

Barger, T.K. "You can go far in this world on kindness." *The Blade*, March 8, 2014.

Brozozowski, Carol. "Beginnings of Buddhism." *Sun Sentinel*, August 19, 1988.

Carrithers, Michael. *Buddha: A Very Short Introduction*. Oxford, England: Oxford University Press, 2001.

Easwaran, Eknath. *Essence of the Dhammapada: The Buddha's Call to Nirvana*. Tomales, CA: Nilgiri Press, 2013.

Graves, Thomas. "Buddha's day, 25 centuries later." *The Sun* (Baltimore), May 2, 1988.

Herold, Andre Ferdinand. *The Life of Buddha*. Amazon Digital Services, 2010.

Kerouac, Jack. *Wake Up*. New York: Viking, 2008 (reprint).

Kumar, Siddhartha. "India to hold caste-based census next year." *McClatchy-Tribune Business News*, September 9, 2010.

Meissonnier, Martin (director). *The Life of Buddha*. Arte, 2004.

Nelson, Walter Henry. *Buddha: His Life and His Teaching*. New York: Penguin, 1996.

PBS, *The Living Edens*. http://www.pbs.org/edens/thailand/buddhism.htm

Strong, John S. *The Buddha: A Short Biography*. Oxford, England: One World, 2001.

Wise, Sarah. "Saturday review: Arts—Secrets of the Buddha." *The Guardian*, April 27, 2002.

PHONETIC PRONUNCIATIONS

Ashoka (a-SHOH-ka)
Asita (a-SEE-tuh)
Dandapani
  (dan-da-PAH-nee)
Devadutta
  (dev-uh-DUH-tuh)
Kapilavastu
  (KAP-i-la-vahs-too)
Mayadevi (my-uh-DEV-ee)

Pajapati Gotami (pa-juh-
  PAH-tee go-TAH-mee)
Rahula (rah-HOO-la)
Siddhartha Gautama (sid-
  AR-thuh gah-TAH-muh)
Sudhodana
  (sud-oh-DAH-na)
Yashodhara
  (ya-shoh-DAH-ra)

Buddhist temple at Koh Samui, Thailand

PHOTO CREDITS: Cover, p. 1—2p2play/Thinkstock; pp. 4, 31—Nomu420/cc-by-sa 3.0; p. 6—Sanand1985/Dreamstime; p. 7—davidevison/Thinkstock; pp. 8–9—myself/cc-by-sa 2.5; p. 10—Christopher Michel/cc-by 2.0; p. 11—Mhoo1990/Thinkstock; p. 12—Jean-Marie Hullot/cc-by 3.0; pp. 14–15—Yves Picq/cc-by-sa 3.0; p. 16—DiverDave/cc-by-sa 4.0; p. 17—MediaJet/cc-by-sa 3.0; p. 18—National Museum Vietnamese History/Jbarta/cc-by-sa 3.0; p. 19—myself/cc-by-sa 2.5; p. 20—Siksan Panpinyo/Dreamstime; p. 23—Tevaprapas/cc-by 3.0; p. 25—Aliaksandr Mazurkevich/Dreamstime; p. 26—Pzaxe/Dreamstime; pp. 28–29, 34/Hintha/cc-by-sa 3.0; p. 32—Abanindranath Tagore/public domain; p. 35—Sacca/public domain; p. 36—myself/public domain; p. 37—Steve Estvanik/Dreamstime; p. 38—Gunawan Kartapranata/cc-by-sa 3.0; p. 39—M Tracy Hunter/cc-by-sa 3.0; p. 40—coward_lion/Dreamstime; p. 46— Preto_perola/Thinkstock.

adversary (AD-ver-sair-ee)—opponent

archaeology (ahr-kee-AHL-uh-jee)—the science that deals with past human life as shown by relics, monuments and tools left by ancient peoples

astrology (uh-STROL-uh-jee)—the study of the supposed influences of the stars on human affairs by their positions in relation to each other

charnel (CHAHR-nuhl)—associated with death

compassion (kuhm-PASH-uhn)—sorrow or pity toward the suffering or misfortune of others

enlightenment (ehn-LIE-tuhn-muhnt)—pure and unqualified knowledge

entitled (en-TIE-tuhld)—deserving of privileges

haughty (HAW-tee)—rudely proud in a manner that expresses scorn for others

hierarchy (HIE-uhr-ahr-kee)—persons or things arranged in ranks or classes

karma (KAHR-muh)—actions seen as bringing inevitable results upon oneself, good or bad, either in this lifetime or in a reincarnation

meditate (MED-ih-tate)—to spend time in quiet thinking

minister (MIN-uh-ster)—a high official who heads a department of the government

nirvana (nir-VAH-nuh)—freedom from the endless cycle of personal reincarnations

reconcile (REK-uhn-sile)—to bring into agreement or harmony

reincarnation (ree-in-kahr-NAY-shuhn)—rebirth in new bodies or forms of life, especially the rebirth of a soul in a new human body

sage (SAYJ)—a very wise person